born with his dna

born with his dna

Always And Forever A Jew

millie nielsen with coco banken

authorHOUSE®

AuthorHouse™
1663 Liberty Drive
Bloomington, IN 47403
www.authorhouse.com
Phone: 1-800-839-8640

First published by AuthorHouse   09/23/2011

ISBN: 978-1-4670-3667-2 (sc)
ISBN: 978-1-4670-3666-5 (hc)
ISBN: 978-1-4670-3665-8 (ebk)

Library of Congress Control Number: 2011916876

Printed in the United States of America

dedication

This book is dedicated to my three sons; John, Peter, and Paul.

- John died from an aneurysm while living in Florida in 2005.
- Peter and wife, Gillian, live in Fuengirola, Spain.
- Paul and wife, Carol, live in Plymouth, Minnesota, U.S.A.

With gratitude to God, I cherish each member of my family with an everlasting love. I praise God for the gift of their lives.

Dear Reader,

At the age of 96 years young, I joyfully share my life journey with you.

You will see the hand of God in my life as you read this chronology, written to give Him glory.

My recollections are a combination of both cherished and bittersweet memories, and at times, somewhat ambiguous. As you may ascertain, many more events occurred throughout nine and a half decades of living.

A major event occurred when I reached age 83; God gave me a new birth. He revealed to me His own Son, the Messiah, Yeshua (Jesus).

The primary purpose in writing this memoir is my heart's desire to share the Messiah with all mankind – my fellow Jews and the Nations.

God has taught me He is always with me. He is also with you, my friend.

So be encouraged! Our lives are designed by God before we are born.

> *"And in Your book they all were written, the days fashioned for me, when as yet there were none of them."*
>
> ***Psalm 139:16***

What a comforting thought! Nothing surprises Him.

Very early in my childhood I adopted the mindset to *always* be young at heart. With enthusiasm and vigor, I enjoy each day of life. My path is never downhill. I am here on earth for a brief period of time, so

"L'Chaim!" "To life!"

My approach in life is not to judge others. I accept people just as they are. God radiates His love to me. I pay it forward.

I am a Jew.

I was born a Jew.

I will die a Jew. Accepting His Messiah does not change this.

I was Born With His DNA

Read the Bible. Talk to God.

> *"Come now, let us reason together," says the LORD. "Though your sins are like scarlet, they shall be white as snow; they are red as crimson, they shall be like wool!"*
>
> *Isaiah 1:18*

Listen to God.

contents

united kingdom

chapter 1

Bamber Street In Liverpool

My earthly life began on March 17, 1915 in Liverpool, England, the third of five children born to Goodman (Guido) Tvergo and Jane Dora Stein Tvergo (Devorah Stein).

Delivered at our home at 102 Bamber Street by my maternal grandmother, who earned her living as midwife for the Orthodox Jewish community, I was a first generation Brit. Both of my parents were immigrants.

Born in the Ukraine, Mother was a devout Orthodox Jew. Her family was financially poor, yet had a rich religious heritage and deep faith in God. She was seventeen years old when her family arrived from the Ukraine.

Born in Kovno, Lithuania, Father was a secular Jew. His prominent family was financially wealthy, yet lacked the religious tradition of our forefathers. The Tvergo family was renowned for their generous philanthropy. Father was four years old when his family arrived from Lithuania.

When my parents came to England with their families in the early part of the twentieth century, the goal of these settlers was to avoid the pogroms of Eastern Europe. They emigrated from their homelands prior to the Bolshevik Revolution, when common citizens revolted against the tyranny of Russian Czar Nicholas II, whose power and influence permeated throughout the Eastern European regions.

Previous to World War I, which began in 1914 with the assassination of Archduke Franz Ferdinand of Austria, resident Jews were increasingly despised in many nations. Because England treated Jews more favorably, my ancestors believed it was a logical choice for establishing a new homeland for posterity.

Upon arrival in their newly adopted country, the immigrants assimilated into ethnic neighborhoods to settle their families, master trades and professions, and establish businesses and commercial enterprises.

Jewish tradition dictated that a matchmaker arrange marriages. The union of my parents, Goodman and Jane Dora, was thus arranged and agreed upon by both families.

It was not a good match; not built on love. It combined two individuals who had dissimilar agendas and differing dreams and aspirations for their lifetime together. Consequently, the relationship between my mother and my father was often tumultuous.

I believe my sad, unhappy childhood was formulated as a result of the turmoil within our home. In retrospect, I realize because Mother felt unloved by her husband, she was unable to express love to me in the manner I needed to receive love as a young child.

Mother was a wounded soul from this arranged marriage. Her disappointment and emotional pain made it nearly impossible for her to demonstrate affection or verbalize love to her children. Still, I loved Mother dearly and never stopped craving her love in return. Deep within I knew she loved all of her family.

Unselfish in every way, Mother labored incessantly and rarely rested. She worked hard and was devoted to caring for her family in spite of physical illness. Mother was diabetic and often suffered the symptoms of the disease.

Mother was my inspiration.

She repaired our worn shoes and sewed our garments. Out of meager means, she cooked nutritious kosher food for our meals, while keeping a clean and organized home.

Mother exemplified selflessness, yet as far as I know, she never knew the Messiah. Still, I pray I will see her again in the golden city, the New Jerusalem. I will never stop loving her and cherishing her memory.

Family communication within our home was minimal. Absent an intense, awkward silence, our home life was often a battleground. Hence, the years of my youth were very difficult.

Fear controlled me as a child. At times it paralyzed me. I was fearful of everything, perceiving myself a misfit within my family and the entire world.

As I reflect upon my sad childhood, I am unsure of whether I was born with innate fear or whether it developed as a result of my living environment. I considered myself inadequate; not good enough and having no worth. Others seemed to possess more value.

Part of my insecurity was caused by my father's attitude toward girls.

One day my father told me that when I was born, he wanted to throw me out with the trash. He said, *"Who wanted another girl?"*

I was devastated.

My parents had four daughters and one son. Fanny was the oldest, the second Sybil, and I was the third daughter. Finally, Maurice arrived! He was the only son born to Goodman and Jane Dora.

How special it is, in Jewish tradition, to have a son. Indeed, it is a favored blessing. Maurice was followed by the youngest daughter, Pearl.

Our neighborhood on Bamber Street was comprised of Eastern European immigrants; Russians, Poles, Lithuanians, various other Eastern Europeans. We were a Jewish ghetto; part of the city of Liverpool, yet a people group separate onto ourselves. In the outside world we did not emphasize anything Jewish, because that would be like donning a bull's eye in the anti-Semitic society of those times.

With three adults and five children inhabiting our small rented home, living quarters were quite crowded. My maternal grandmother came to live with us to assist Mother in caring for Sybil, who had contracted polio. Much time was spent treating Sybil, and Mother was exhausted.

Because anti-Semitism was rampant in Europe, we Anglicized our names for the outside world. The days were rife with fear. Grandmother addressed us by our Hebrew names only while inside our home; Fanny was Feagala, Sybil was Sarah, I was Michala, Maurice was Moshe, and Pearl was Pia.

As a child, I often withdrew to the attic to be alone, thinking no one wanted me around. At mealtime, Mother would call me to the table but my sisters would say, *"Just leave her be."*

Oh, how I wished they would want me to be a part of the family! I felt so excluded, so lonely. If only they would have coaxed me in the slightest, then I would have known they wanted my presence.

My childhood fears increased as I grew older; fear of the dark, fear of water, fear of thunder, fear of people, fear of being alone, fear of being inadequate . . . just fear of everything. Life was so unpleasant.

Above all, I hated being Jewish. At home we were taught we were God's chosen people. Why, then, did God allow us to be targeted? It did not compute in my mind.

Jews were hated.

I hated *being* a Jew.

I hid my identity all my life, until I met Yeshua at age 83.

- New Brighton, Bathing Pool
- New Brighton, Vale Park Bandstand
- New Brighton, Sands and Promenade

These photographs of New Brighton, Wallasey, are from a postcard I have saved since my childhood. They are most probably from the early part of the 20th century.

New Brighton is across the Mersey from Liverpool.

- New Brighton, Pier and Ferry
- New Brighton from the Pier
- New Brighton from the Pier

Liverpool is my birthplace.

England is my homeland.

America is my new home, and I am so grateful to God to be an American citizen.

chapter 2

Life As An Orthodox Jew

Mother was a devout woman of God. She strived to *"Train up a child in the way he should go, and when he is old, he will not depart from it,"* as written in Proverbs 22:6. She was diligent in her efforts to be an observant Jew and to raise her children in the tradition of our ancestors. Grandmother helped maintain Orthodox Judaic teaching in our home.

But in the outside world, every member of the family was careful not to expose or talk about our Judaism. Jews were hated in most of Europe. Their businesses in Liverpool were regularly vandalized; windows were broken, and swastikas and other graffiti were painted on buildings.

Again, at home we were continually reminded we were *"God's chosen people; a royal priesthood, a holy nation."* Mother said we were targeted because others were jealous. I was confused and did not understand the situation. Like the character, Tevye the milkman, in the play, *Fiddler on the Roof,* (based on the Yiddish creative writings of <u>Sholom Aleichem</u>), I thought, *"So we are Your chosen people. Why didn't You choose someone else?"*

Oh, how I hated being Jewish! I pretended not to be a Jew. When I read books or whenever the thought occurred to me, I would push up the tip of my aquiline nose so I would resemble a Gentile.

As observant Jews, we attended shul (synagogue) regularly. I did not particularly like the services because they were in Hebrew and I didn't understand what was spoken or sung.

Faithfully, Mother walked all five of us children to Sabbath services each week. Many times our grandmother also attended services. Father did not attend.

Preparing for Shabbat was very important to Mother. Like observant Jewish families around the world, we prepared to *"Keep holy the Sabbath."* Actually, in Jewish tradition, observing Shabbat is more sacred than Yom Kippur (the Day of Atonement—the holiest day of the year). Leviticus 23:3 states: *"There are six days when you may work, but the seventh day is a day of Sabbath rest, a day of sacred assembly. You are not to do any work; where you live, it is a Sabbath to the Lord."*

Called Erev Shabbat (evening before Sabbath), it begins each Friday at 18 minutes before sunset with a beautiful candle lighting ceremony and special prayers.

Two small Sabbath candles (which burn approximately three hours) are lit by the veil-covered mother or matriarch of the family. The father or patriarch blesses wine and challah (three-strand braided bread). He reads Proverbs 31 about *"a righteous woman,"* and thanks the Almighty for the gift of his wife.

Shabbat candles must be lit before sunset. To light candles after sunset is considered a desecration of the Sabbath.

Though English is read from left to right, Hebrew is read from right to left.

Candle Blessing

(Prayed by the mother or matriarch after she lights the two Sabbath candles, circling her hands toward her face three times to indicate the acceptance and sanctity of Shabbat, then covering her eyes while reciting)

בָּרוּךְ אַתָּה יְיָ אֱלֹהֵינוּ מֶלֶךְ הָעוֹלָם

Barukh atah Adonai, Eloheinu, melekh ha'olam
Blessed are you, Lord, our God, sovereign of the universe

אֲשֶׁר קִדְּשָׁנוּ בְּמִצְוֹתָיו וְצִוָּנוּ

asher kidishanu b'mitz'votav v'tzivanu
Who has sanctified us with His commandments and
commanded us

לְהַדְלִיק נֵר שֶׁל שַׁבָּת : (אָמֵן)

l'had'lik neir shel Shabbat. (Amein) to light the lights of
Shabbat. (Amen)

(The mother then uncovers her eyes and beholds the Shabbat lights.)

Kiddush Blessing

(Recited by the father or patriarch while holding a cup of wine or grape juice)

נַיְהִי עֶרֶב נַיְהִי בֹקֶר יוֹם הַשִּׁשִּׁי

Vay'hi erev vay'hi voker yom hashishi
And there was evening and there was morning, a sixth day

וַיְכֻלּוּ הַשָּׁמַיִם וְהָאָרֶץ וְכָל צְבָאָם

vay'khulu hashamayim v'ha'aretz v'khol tz'va'am
The heavens and the earth were finished, the whole host of them

וַיְכַל אֱלֹהִים בַּיּוֹם הַשְּׁבִיעִי מְלַאכְתּוֹ אֲשֶׁר עָשָׂה

vay'khal elohim bayom hash'vi'i m'la'kh'to asher asah
And on the seventh day God completed his work that he had done

וַיְבָרֶךְ אֱלֹהִים אֶת יוֹם הַשְּׁבִיעִי בַיְקַדֵּשׁ אֹתוֹ

Vay'varekh Elohim et yom hash'vi'i vay'kadeish oto
And God blessed the seventh day, and sanctified it

כִּי בוֹ שָׁבַת מִכָּל מְלַאכְתּוֹ אֲשֶׁר בָּרָא אֱלֹהִים לַעֲשׂוֹת

ki vo shavat mikol m'la'kh'to asher bara Elohim la'asot because in it he had rested from all his work that God had created to do

בָּרוּךְ אַתָּה יְיָ אֱלֹהֵינוּ מֶלֶךְ הָעוֹלָם

Barukh atah Adonai, Eloheinu, melekh ha-olam
Blessed are you, Lord, our God, sovereign of the universe

בּוֹרֵא פְּרִי הַגָּפֶן (אָמֵן)

borei p'ri hagafen (Amein)
Who creates the fruit of the vine (Amen)

בָּרוּךְ אַתָּה יְיָ אֱלֹהֵינוּ מֶלֶךְ הָעוֹלָם

Barukh atah Adonai, Eloheinu, melekh ha-olam
Blessed are You, Lord, our God, King of the Universe

אֲשֶׁר קִדְּשָׁנוּ בְּמִצְוֹתָיו וְרָצָה בָנוּ

asher kid'shanu b'mitz'votav v'ratzah vanu who sanctifies us with
his commandments, and has been pleased with us

וְשַׁבַּת קָדְשׁוֹ בְּאַהֲבָה וּבְרָצוֹן הִנְחִילָנוּ זִכָּרוֹן לְמַעֲשֵׂה בְרֵאשִׁית

*v'shabat kad'sho b'ahavah uv'ratzon hin'chilanu zikaron
l'ma'aseih v'rei'shit*
You have lovingly and willingly given us Your holy Shabbat as
an inheritance, in memory of creation

כִּי הוּא יוֹם תְּחִלָּה לְמִקְרָאֵי קֹדֶשׁ זֵכֶר לִיצִיאַת מִצְרָיִם

ki hu yom t'chilah l'mik'ra'ei kodesh zeikher litzi'at Mitz'rayim
because it is the first day of our holy assemblies, in memory of
the exodus from Egypt

כִּי בָנוּ בָחַרְתָּ וְאוֹתָנוּ קִדַּשְׁתָּ מִכָּל הָעַמִּים

ki vanu vachar'ta v'otanu kidash'ta mikol ha'amim because You
have chosen us and made us holy from all peoples

וְשַׁבַּת קָדְשְׁךָ בְּאַהֲבָה וּבְרָצוֹן הִנְחַלְתָּנוּ

v'shabat kad'sh'kha b'ahavah uv'ratzon hin'chal'tanu and have
willingly and lovingly given us Your holy Shabbat for an
inheritance

בָּרוּךְ אַתָּה יְיָ מְקַדֵּשׁ הַשַּׁבָּת (אָמֵן)

Barukh atah Adonai m'kadeish hashabat (Amein)
Blessed are You, who sanctifies Shabbat (Amen)

13

אֲשֶׁר קִדְּשָׁנוּ בְּמִצְוֹתָיו וְרָצָה בָנוּ

asher kid'shanu b'mitz'votav v'ratzah vanu who sanctifies us with his commandments, and has been pleased with us

וְשַׁבַּת קָדְשׁוֹ בְּאַהֲבָה וּבְרָצוֹן הִנְחִילָנוּ זִכָּרוֹן לְמַעֲשֵׂה בְרֵאשִׁית

v'shabat kad'sho b'ahavah uv'ratzon hin'chilanu zikaron l'ma'aseih v'rei'shit

You have lovingly and willingly given us Your holy Shabbat as an inheritance, in memory of creation

כִּי הוּא יוֹם תְּחִלָּה לְמִקְרָאֵי קֹדֶשׁ זֵכֶר לִיצִיאַת מִצְרָיִם

ki hu yom t'chilah l'mik'ra'ei kodesh zeikher litzi'at Mitz'rayim

because it is the first day of our holy assemblies, in memory of the exodus from Egypt

כִּי בָנוּ בָחַרְתָּ וְאוֹתָנוּ קִדַּשְׁתָּ מִכָּל הָעַמִּים

ki vanu vachar'ta v'otanu kidash'ta mikol ha'amim because You have chosen us and made us holy from all peoples

וְשַׁבַּת קָדְשְׁךָ בְּאַהֲבָה וּבְרָצוֹן הִנְחַלְתָּנוּ

v'shabat kad'sh'kha b'ahavah uv'ratzon hin'chal'tanu and have willingly and lovingly given us Your holy Shabbat for an inheritance

בָּרוּךְ אַתָּה יְיָ מְקַדֵּשׁ הַשַּׁבָּת (אָמֵן)

Barukh atah Adonai m'kadeish hashabat (Amein).
Blessed are You, who sanctifies Shabbat (Amen)

Washing Hands

(After Kiddush and before the meal, each person in the household should wash hands by filling a cup with water and pouring it over the top and bottom of the right hand and then the left hand. Before wiping the hands dry on a towel, the following blessing is recited.)

בָּרוּךְ אַתָּה יְיָ אֱלֹהֵינוּ מֶלֶךְ הָעוֹלָם

Barukh atah Adonai, Eloheinu, melekh ha-olam
Blessed are You, Lord, our God, King of the Universe

אֲשֶׁר קִדְּשָׁנוּ בְּמִצְוֹתָיו וְצִוָּנוּ

asher kidishanu b'mitz'votav v'tzivanu
Who has sanctified us with His commandments and commanded us

עַל נְטִילַת יָדָיִם

al n'tilat yadayim.
concerning washing of hands.

There is no "Amen" at the end of this blessing. Traditionally, each person washes their own hands and says their own blessing. A leader says the blessing on behalf of everyone; then all others say "Amen."

15

Ha Motzi Blessing

Immediately after washing hands and before eating, the head of the household should remove the cover from the two challah loaves, lifting them while reciting the following blessing.

בָּרוּךְ אַתָּה יְיָ אֱלֹהֵינוּ מֶלֶךְ הָעוֹלָם

Barukh atah Adonai, Eloheinu, melekh ha-olam

Blessed are You, Lord, our God, King of the Universe

הַמּוֹצִיא לֶחֶם מִן הָאָרֶץ (אָמֵן)

hamotzi lechem min ha'aretz. (Amein).

who brings forth bread from the earth. (Amen)

The challah is then ripped into pieces or sliced and passed around the table, so that each person may have a piece. The family meal may then begin.

These Friday night prayers and traditions are a weekly reminder of the blessings of faith and family. Following this ceremony, everyone sits at the table to dine.

At our home each Friday night, Father came reluctantly to the dinner table. He could not wait for it to end. He was most uncomfortable with Sabbath tradition.

- Our Friday ritual included:
- Advance preparation of Sabbath meals
- Table setting with a special white damask tablecloth used only for Shabbat
- Silver candleholders holding new Sabbath candles which always burn to the end (Jews never extinguish a candle—never put out a light except ceremonially to end Sabbath)
- Our finest china and silver
- The silver Kiddush cup for wine as part of the Sabbath blessings
- Fresh flowers that Mother *always* insisted adorn the table

The ambiance at Shabbat supper is joyful, with a holiness and reverence of God and enriched communication with one another. With honoring God comes honoring one another.

Part of our Sabbath preparation meant ensuring our best clothes were clean and pressed and our shoes were polished for shul. We were always impeccably dressed in our best attire when Mother walked us to the synagogue on *Shabbat* morning. We each had one outfit for Sabbath.

This tradition is similar in all observant Jewish homes throughout the world. The Sabbath is a gift from God. Celebrating this gift is a demonstration of gratitude to our Abba Father for His innumerable blessings and for His gift of rest.

Sabbath worship was a priority for Mother in teaching her children to honor God. Wearing our best clothes was showing respect to our Maker.

Mother painstakingly sewed little green velvet jackets for her four daughters to wear to shul. They were soft and lovely, so warm in the moist Liverpool air. I always enjoyed dressing up and looking pretty. The soft velvet made me feel very good.

The warmth of that memory is tainted by sadness when I remember the slurs directed at us as we walked to and from the synagogue. Some called us *"dirty Jews"* and *"Christ killers."* We always felt safer once we were back in our homes.

In observance of the Sabbath, Jews are forbidden to do any unnecessary labor. So every Saturday, a Gentile girl would come into each of the Jewish dwellings up and down Bamber Street and shuttle coal into the stoves, to keep the fires burning so our homes remained heated. By Saturday evening it was often very cold in the house as the embers burned down.

The Sabbath ends on Saturday night after three stars appear in the night sky (approximately forty-five minutes after sunset) with another traditional candle lighting ceremony and prayers called *Havdalah.*

We ended our Sabbath with the Havdalah ceremony and then once again were free to cook and light a fire—to labor once again.

A three-wick braided candle is lit, wine is poured into the Kiddush cup, and a spice blend is passed for all to smell—to savor the aromas of life. After this portion the father prays a thanksgiving prayer for the gift of Shabbat, the day of rest. He extinguishes the candle in the wine by tipping it upside down and touching the flame in the liquid. Then Sabbath is officially ended.

After this ceremony is completed, the family often cooks and then dines together, enjoying the cholent (stew), which has been kept warm on a jockey board.

There is a natural stress release that occurs when fulfillment of the command to observe the Sabbath is completed. The ambiance is relaxed and everyone is jovial and talkative.

Kiddush Blessing

בָּרוּךְ אַתָּה יְיָ אֱלֹהֵינוּ מֶלֶךְ הָעוֹלָם

Barukh atah Adonai, Eloheinu, melekh ha'olam

Blessed are you, Lord, our God, sovereign of the universe

בּוֹרֵא פְּרִי הַגָּפֶן (אָמֵן)

borei p'ri hagafen (Amein)

Who creates the fruit of the vine (Amen)

Spices Blessing

בָּרוּךְ אַתָּה יְיָ אֱלֹהֵינוּ מֶלֶךְ הָעוֹלָם
בּוֹרֵא מִינֵי בְשָׂמִים (אָמֵן)

Barukh atah Adonai, Eloheinu, melekh ha'olam, borei minei v'samim
(Amein)

Blessed are you, Lord, our God, sovereign of the universe,
Who creates varieties of spices (Amen)

Candle Blessing

בָּרוּךְ אַתָּה יְיָ אֱלֹהֵינוּ מֶלֶךְ הָעוֹלָם

Barukh atah Adonai, Eloheinu, melekh ha'olam

Blessed are you, Lord, our God, sovereign of the universe

בּוֹרֵא מְאוֹרֵי הָאֵשׁ (אָמֵן)

borei m'orei ha'eish (Amein)

Who creates the light of the fire (Amen)

Havdalah Blessing

בָּרוּךְ אַתָּה יְיָ אֱלֹהֵינוּ מֶלֶךְ הָעוֹלָם

Barukh atah Adonai, Eloheinu, melekh ha'olam
Blessed are you, Lord, our God, sovereign of the universe

הַמַּבְדִּיל בֵּין קֹדֶשׁ לְחוֹל

hamav'dil bein kodesh l'chol
Who separates between sacred and secular

בֵּין אוֹר לְחֹשֶׁךְ בֵּין יִשְׂרָאֵל לָעַמִּים

bein or l'choshekh bein Yis'ra'eil la'amim
between light and darkness, between Israel and the nations

בֵּין יוֹם הַשְּׁבִיעִי לְשֵׁשֶׁת יְמֵי הַמַּעֲשֶׂה

bein yom hash'vi'i l'sheishet y'mei hama'aseh
between the seventh day and the six days of labor

בָּרוּךְ אַתָּה יְיָ הַמַּבְדִּיל בֵּין קֹדֶשׁ לְחוֹל

Barukh atah Adonai, hamav'dil bein kodesh l'chol (Amein).
Blessed are You, Lord, who separates between sacred and secular. (Amen)

I recall the comfort of sitting by the fire at Sabbath's end, keeping warm while snuggled at the hearth, enjoying the aroma of delicious simmering food. It was a pleasant feeling in the misty Liverpool climate to allow your body to warm back up after feeling chilled to the bone.

Sunday was often the day when friends and extended family shared time together. Neighborhood children played games, either in one of the homes or outside, while adults and teenagers engaged in conversation.

On Monday, my weekly responsibility was to take the damask tablecloth to the Chinese laundry so it would be ready for the following Friday. I was terrified of this task.

After rushing to arrive at the laundry, I stood trembling at the entrance. The polite Chinese man smiled as he walked over to the doorway and gently took the tablecloth from my arms. Then I turned and ran home as fast as possible.

This happened week after week. Though he was a kind and gentle man, I never stopped being afraid. He looked different.

It was war time and there were Black soldiers in Liverpool. I was terrified of them, also, because they looked different.

chapter 3

Living With Father's Addiction

My paternal grandfather died when I was a toddler. I was told he was a good man, a man of high society, greatly esteemed in the community. As a wealthy philanthropist, he generously donated to Jewish schools and Jewish charities.

Father was youngest of his five children. I was told that Grandfather had hated his son's attitude.

Perhaps my own father did not accept leadership responsibilities and was not dedicated to providing for his family because of low self-esteem. Unable to measure up to the high standards of his heritage, he subsequently became addicted to gambling. Father was narcissistic, a pleasure-seeker, hoping for big winnings.

From Mother's perspective, Father was totally unreliable. She worried about his gambling addiction. Many times on payday she would go to his workplace to retrieve some of his earnings to buy food and coal before Father gambled away everything at the racetrack. Horseracing was Father's passion.

As a child, I physically felt the tension between my parents. The pervasive stress in our family is a vivid memory to me.

Because Father was often visibly present but emotionally absent, Mother felt compelled to meet the demands of both parental roles. She was a wonderful woman, a good mother, but the stress took a toll on her health and continual strife robbed her of joy. While suffering with diabetes, her daily challenges included coping with an irresponsible husband, raising five children, and caring for a child with polio. There is little wonder she was unhappy.

In addition to all the burdens she carried, Mother took in ironing and mending to supplement family income. She even raised chickens in our backyard for extra revenue.

On Friday mornings, Mother took chickens to a kosher slaughterhouse to have the birds butchered properly in a manner called Shechita. Then back at home, Mother and Grandmother plucked out the feathers. When ready for cooking, the chickens were sold to neighbors and one was kept for our Shabbat meal.

In those times of my childhood, the world was in turmoil. Now I look back at the difficulties we lived through and thank God for my mother. She loved God and did her very best in spite of tremendous hardship and undesirable circumstances. She loved us and desired a better life for her family.

We all admired Mother. She taught us responsibility by her example, and we learned to always persevere.

Often Mother was disappointed and hurt by Father's actions. I recall one occasion when Father took the lovely velvet jackets Mother had sewn for her daughters to wear to synagogue, and pawned them for gambling money.

Mother was devastated!

What a breach of trust for Father to take Sabbath clothes away from his children to feed his addiction.

I was crushed to learn my lovely velvet jacket was gone.

chapter 4

The Scholarship

During the early part of the twentieth century, grammar schools in England enrolled children aged 4 through 14 years of age.

The first time I remember feeling contented with myself was when I was 11 years old. I attended Hebrew School in Liverpool, as did my siblings and all of the Jewish children in our neighborhood.

At Hebrew School, two academic scholarships were awarded annually to students in their fifth year of middle grammar study; one to a boy and one to a girl. Named for their benefactor, the Isidore Silverberg Scholarships were awarded primarily for academics, although additional criteria were used to evaluate students and to select recipients.

Apparently I found favor with the Selection Committee, because I was awarded the girl's scholarship. As a special gift, I was given a prized book by the Hebrew School.

This achievement was a huge highlight for me. It gave me a reason to finally experience joy in an otherwise sad and lonely childhood. I began to view myself with a higher level of respect and esteem.

The scholarship award event was exhilarating. I was paraded throughout the entire school to each of the classrooms. In each room the headmaster announced my award to all of the students, who smiled and applauded me. What joy filled my heart!

My grandmother was especially excited about this award. She grinned from ear to ear as she told neighbors and friends of the honor bestowed upon me. Even my siblings and parents were proud of me. I was elated.

This was a boost I desperately needed. I believe with all my heart the hand of God was upon this honor. It was a turning point in my life.

Because of this scholarship, I left Hebrew School early, at age 12, to attend Oulten Secondary Academy for the subsequent four years.

As excited and delighted as I was upon entering the Academy, I soon realized the economic inconsistencies among the students. The vast majority of my peers came from wealthy professional families. Tuition to this private school was expensive.

Our school uniforms were attractive. They included a white shirt, black tunic, and black tam hat, along with uniform socks and shoes.

The new clothes of the wealthy students were bright, crisp and pressed. The uniforms given to me were handed down from others; well worn, faded, and permanently wrinkled. My uniform socks had holes worn in the heels, so I would pull the toes of the socks forward and fold them under. Then people could not see the holes now hidden in my shoes.

At the Academy, I considered myself an outcast . . . . second class. Yet the other students respected me. They knew I was there on scholarship.

The curriculum at the Academy included business law and economics. The instructors were preparing me for a career in academics or international business.

Most Academy students traveled to France for a portion of their final year of study. I was unable to afford this luxury, as it was not part of the tuition scholarship.

I felt left out. I couldn't compete with wealthy students. While classmates were abroad, I sought an outlet to compensate my feelings of inadequacy.

Since a love of music and dancing was in my soul, I joined a hop (dance club) for a minimal fee. I wanted to learn proper dance steps and technique. The lessons were conveniently scheduled after school hours so it didn't interfere with my studies.

Many male instructors at the hop taught me popular moves and encouraged me to continue dancing, stating I had *"good rhythm."* I LOVED hearing that!

I graduated from the Academy at age 16 and began my career in the business world. To continue advanced education at the University of Liverpool after Oulten Academy would have required an additional scholarship.

A food manufacturer, Melias, offered me a prestigious office position, which I accepted. Many colleagues and contemporaries envied me for receiving the coveted role. It was a career building opportunity. But I soon became unhappy and dissatisfied with the politics of the corporate world.

Again, I hated being Jewish. In an effort to hide this, I worked on high holy days so the Gentiles wouldn't know I was a Jew. I doubt they were fooled, though. I looked like an Ashkenazi (Eastern European) Jew.

Too concerned with other's opinions and consumed with my personal appearance, the focus was entirely on me. I spent a great deal of my earnings on clothes and shoes. Fashion was my idol and I contemplated my image at all times.

Because I always maintained a thin physique and was able to wear clothes well, I longed to appear chic. I had visited Paris, the fashion capital, only while daydreaming!

In my limited perception, I believed style was an outward expression of my success in life; it validated my worth.

chapter 5

My Love Of Dance

Nothing in all of life thrilled me more than dancing. In an elegant evening gown, I felt like a princess as I was whisked across a ballroom floor.

My sister, Sybil, also loved to dance. Though polio left her with a leg which did not grow to full size, she was able to dance and enjoyed it immensely. We both loved to wear beautiful gowns.

Since my first job at Melias paid eight shillings, I split the salary two ways; half I gave to Mother for rent, half went to fabric and sewing expenses for gowns created by Sybil, who was a talented fashion designer. Each week she sewed new gowns for the two of us to wear.

Sybil was apprenticed as couture designer to a dressmaker's shop that was located on a quaint little narrow street in the heart of Liverpool. There she could sit down while working, creating garments and making alterations. Sybil learned to sew from Mother, who was a very talented seamstress.

The dressmaker's shop was located in a shopping district that looked as classic as in a Dickens novel. The district had cobblestone streets, gas streetlamps and multi-paned window fronts and facades. Close in proximity was a millinery shop, a haberdashery for distinguished gentlemen, a watchmaker, a shoemaker, a pipe tobacco shop, and a bread bakery; all fine quality establishments.

Refined women in Liverpool frequented the dress shop where Sybil worked because it was known for offering top quality fabric and designs. Everyone in that era wore clothing that was custom fitted to their particular body shape and form. Clothing was either tailored at home or in a dressmaker's shop; garments were not off the rack. Fashions were custom tailored during the years before mass production methods changed the garment industry.

While dancing in the beautiful gowns created by Sybil, my weekends held glamour, romance, and excitement . . . everything I longed for in life during my late teenage years. Saturday night at the dance, my joy! To reminisce is so pleasant.

Sybil and I felt like wealthy royalty with the multitude of gowns we owned. Since we wore the same dress size, occasionally during mid-evening we met in the ladies powder room at the cotillion to trade gowns. This kept the suitors guessing. We had such fun!

Each weekend I attended a ball. It was the Big Band Era. I was privileged to dance to famous band leaders such as Glenn Miller, Artie Shaw, Harry James, Tommy and Jimmy Dorsey, and other talented musical groups who visited England, as well as many of Britain's own bands.

A favorite venue was Grafton Ballroom, the main arena in Liverpool. It was a fabulous building, with a soft spring floor and revolving bandstand . . . state-of-the-art design.

Since Liverpool is a port city, many lonely sailors and seamen wanted female companionship. Ballrooms were full of handsome dance partners, looking very attractive in their military uniforms. At age 96, I still enjoy seeing men in uniform!

Romance was part of the whirl of a cotillion. Socializing which accompanied the dance brought great enjoyment. Some guys and gals were looking for love, for a life partner. Many just wanted to have fun and escape the realities of impending war.

Mother was quite unhappy with me at this time. She did not appreciate the lifestyle I had chosen. When we talked, she would wag her finger at me and tell me I needed to mend my ways. Mother said I had become a worldly woman.

Deep within me I knew she was right but I continued to rebel. She hated the spaghetti straps and bare backs of some of my dance gowns. Grandmother said I was going out naked. Like Mother, she strongly disapproved.

Yet I felt like a royal princess. Sybil was quite a daring fashion designer.

Music was my escape—my therapy in a difficult world which was continually becoming less tolerant of Jews. Dance was a pleasant diversion and I felt empowered with self-confidence on the dance floor. I virtually lived and breathed to dance!

I still do! Music and dance is in my soul.

chapter 6

Mother's Death

Gradually Mother's health deteriorated. Her strength waned. Though she tried to fight for her life, diabetes destroyed Mother's health. I was not prepared for how grave her condition had become.

In retrospect, I am so grateful I was able to help her; to be available to take her to medical appointments and buy the necessary supplies for her condition. This responsibility, left entirely to me, continued until quite abruptly everything changed.

Seeing Mother one day with a big bowl of water she had heated on the stove, I asked, *"Why do you have hot water?"*

She said there was a carbuncle on her back from the diabetes. I volunteered to apply the hot compress, so Mother slipped her dress to her waist. My heart skipped a beat when I saw that the sore covered almost half of her back. I was shocked. Yet I didn't express my terror to Mother.

Considering the situation, I gently questioned whether it might be appropriate to take her to the hospital. She quite firmly refused and requested I not tell anyone about this. I honored Mother's wishes.

One week after this incident, a day before Yom Kippur, she was admitted to the hospital in Liverpool. Mother was very ill.

I sent a cable to her brother in Wales. He came to Liverpool immediately.

Just before midnight on Yom Kippur, I came downstairs and sat on a chair by the dining table, pondering the situation. Just then my uncle walked in, returning from the hospital. He was carrying Mother's clothes. She died on Yom Kippur.

I was utterly devastated.

I lost my mother, whom I loved. She was my best friend.

chapter 7

My Search For Love

With Mother's passing I experienced enormous loss. I felt emptiness within my soul and tremendous guilt for not listening to her advice concerning choices about my lifestyle. Feeling more alone than ever, I was desperately longing for acceptance; for the love I felt eluded me since birth. Grief was my daily companion.

While dancing at the ballroom, I was attracted to a handsome man named George Brereton. His family owned a wireless shop in New Brighton. We danced with each other almost exclusively and spent a lot of time together over the ensuing months. George told me incessantly how much he loved me.

On a Christmas Eve date, he took me to Midnight Mass at his Roman Catholic Church. Although his family was there, we arrived late and they barely noticed me in the darkness of the candlelit church. The service was strange for me and I felt weirdly guilty when we had to kneel.

I really thought I loved this man. We continued to dance and go out to eat after the dance ended. Our relationship eventually went beyond dancing.

At 22 years of age, I was pregnant. Naturally I assumed that the father of my child would marry me because so many times he had professed his love for me. Yet when I told him about the baby I was carrying, he quickly cooled off our relationship and abandoned me. He said he would not consider marrying a Jew.

Mother had been correct in chastening me. I just had not heeded her warnings and was now unwed and pregnant.

Once again I was devastated, this time with guilt, shame, loneliness, _and_ a broken heart. But already feeling protective of the baby growing inside me, I determined to persevere.

During this era in England, women stopped working when their pregnancy began to show. I quit my job in the sixth month. No one said anything to me or asked me to leave. It was just an unwritten law that you ceased employment when you were pregnant.

There were many rumors about me. The whispering always stopped whenever I entered a room.

My father told me that I was no longer welcome at home. My siblings didn't support me either and they told me to move out.

This was unequivocally one of the most difficult periods in my life. The loss of home and family, rejection by the man I loved, along with anticipated new responsibilities of motherhood, was all overwhelming.

Still grieving the loss of my beloved mother, pregnant, entrenched in guilt and disappointment, only the love for my baby enabled me to move forward.

Because of my circumstances, I tried to get financial assistance through the English legal system from the father of my child. He refused to pay anything although he admitted the child was his.

Initially I received nothing from him, but eventually the courts ensured I received some compensation. Then George abruptly refused to pay any more. So the courts incarcerated him for debt.

Soon after his incarceration, England was attacked by the Nazis. Prisoners were taken out of jail for military service. George was assigned to active military duty in a war zone.

Shortly thereafter he was killed in action.

chapter 8

The Birth Of My Son

In 1938, I gave birth to a son and named him John Donald (JD, like my mother, Jane Dora). Love for this precious child just filled my heart. The joy of holding him in my arms compensated for all of the previous grief.

Desperate again, I was a homeless single mother with an infant to support. A neighborhood acquaintance, a friend of Mother's, told me of a Christian woman named Madge, who was a waitress. Madge and her husband might allow me to move into their home and live with their family. They had two small children.

After meeting with Madge and discussing the arrangement, she and her family took me in. Her generosity was such a blessing! Even though she was poor and worked very hard, this Christian woman chose to help me and my baby. During these war times life was especially difficult for everyone, including this kind lady. I was amazed at her unselfishness.

Madge's generosity contrasted with my family's rejection. Were kindness and love attributes of a genuine Christian? Even Mother's wealthy brothers had refused to help her financially when she asked. Rather, they contributed large sums to the synagogue where their names would be written on plaques. In fairness to them, they perhaps did not want to enable Father's gambling addiction.

I returned to my employer, Melias, leaving John with a friend who cared for him while I worked. One day after work I picked up John and returned to the Christian family's home where I was staying. I marveled at her earnings as I watched Madge count her tips. She had a lot of shillings!

Since I was not fond of my current position in the manufacturing industry, I inquired about waitressing. I told her I was unhappy in my business career and wanted something different. Also, I wanted more income to get my own flat, raise my son, and enjoy occasional entertainment; specifically, dancing.

Madge talked to her employer, who hired me as a waitress at his upscale restaurant owned by the Greek consulate in Liverpool. The prestigious restaurant served top gourmet cuisine.

During my first day as a waitress I did everything wrong and trembled in fear!

The method of service provided at this establishment was called French service. Wearing dress uniforms with white gloves and carrying a towel draped over our left arm, we served wealthy professionals who dined on candlelit tables with white linen tablecloths, linen napkins, crystal stemware, polished silver, and fine china embossed with the country seal of Greece.

Management was so fastidious. They examined our hands and fingernails before we gloved for service. We were expected to be at our very best at all times.

Our clientele were the upper echelon of Greek and English business. They feasted upon the finest foods and imbibed in expensive wines and liqueurs.

The restaurant served fancy entrees such as Kotopoulo Lemonato (chicken with lemon) and Bakaliaros Tighanitos (fried cod). Taking the entrée from a silver serving platter using a large spoon and fork, we served from the right and removed dishes from the left. Everything was very proper.

My first day, I did everything wrong! Everything! Yet Andre, the maitre d', told me, *"You made a lot of mistakes but don't give up."*

All the while I served that day, the manager was watching me and miraculously decided to keep me on staff and train me properly.

In retrospect, I see this was the hand of God. The experience taught me that I *loved* serving others! It was so gratifying and I felt fulfilled. What joy it was to interact with people and give them a reason to smile.

After working at this establishment for five years, I became the dining room supervisor.

I still love to serve. I am serving my Master, Yeshua.

The Christian woman helped me in so many ways. Surely God designed our paths to cross so I could experience the unselfish love of Jesus through this woman.

With my Christian Friend

With John, my son

chapter 9

The Blitzkrieg

After Mother died, Father moved from Bamber Street to a smaller home on Grove Street. Two sisters and my brother shared accommodations with him.

My family was compassionate. Because they fell in love with John, they wanted him around as much as possible. Previously I was asked to leave home; now I was invited to return. Children are the best ambassadors!

In the cold winter month of February in 1940, John and I moved into my family's three-story, brown brick home.

Our salon (sitting room) was especially inviting and cozy, for while Mother was still alive and we lived on Bamber Street, I convinced her to sew new window treatments and a sofa slipcover on her Singer sewing machine.

Since I loved exciting and dramatic design, I selected and purchased enough fabric for redecorating. The monochromatic pattern had a contemporary design and the color was a bright orange, very bold for that era. The room felt warm, inviting, and modern. Every visitor commented favorably.

Mother was a meticulous seamstress. The fitted slipcover was flawless and the sofa appeared to be tightly upholstered.

The draperies had insulated lining, which kept the room warmer when they were drawn and blocked sunlight, preventing fading on other pieces of furniture. Homes in England had standard window sizes, so the draperies from Bamber Street precisely fit the windows on Grove Street.

On weekends I continued to dance, but seriously mended my ways. Mother was right. I learned a hard lesson in life. Still, God gave me a precious son, even in my disobedience.

John was my joy. I had a difficult time forgiving myself, but I believe God knew I was sorry. I somehow knew that He had forgiven me. God gave me the greatest blessing in my life—a child.

When I attended dances, my father or siblings watched John. They welcomed the opportunity and never complained. John was the center of attention during our gatherings, a catalyst. We all laughed at his silly antics and enjoyed his bubbly personality.

At the ballroom, sailors and seamen often wanted more than just dance, but I had become fiercely independent. Whenever I danced, I insisted upon paying my own expenses. I would never again be indebted to any man. I would not repeat my mistake.

As bombings continued in England, Liverpool had continual blackouts. In the regular evening attacks on this port city, alarms rang, lights were turned out, and everyone ran to bomb shelters. Whenever a target was hit, buildings shook, the ground trembled, fires burned. Air raid sirens screeched their warnings for citizens to hustle to safety.

Most nights we slept in the shelter, sitting in total darkness. In the early light of morning, we returned to our homes to freshen up and dress for work. One of my family members always managed to grab a pillow to take to the shelter for John to lie on as they held him on their lap.

Our lives continued this way during the two years of attacks from the Nazis. I cannot express the terror, living through war on your own homeland.

One morning after leaving the shelter with John in my arms, I saw that that my neighbors, my good friends, failed to make it to the safety of the bomb shelter. Their bodies and body parts were strewn across the garden. It was awful! Terrible! Horrifying!

Not wanting John to experience this horrendous sight while I carried him, I turned his face to look into my eyes as I talked to him, and then tucked his head into my neck as I ran inside our home.

With a cringing pain in the pit of my stomach, I changed my clothes and dressed John for the day. The vivid picture of my neighbors remained in my mind. I forced myself to go to my workplace but I was unable to eat the entire day and barely accomplished anything. For several months I had nightmares recalling this scene.

No one in England talked about the war. We persevered through our daily routines while praying for victory. What a difficult era this was!

Known as the 'bulldog,' Prime Minister Winston Churchill was our hero in England. His stalwart attitude and resolute speeches helped us to remain positive and hopeful. As we listened to him speak on the radio, we felt great pride in England. He encouraged us with resolve to fight and win, for good to triumph over evil. He said that we would never accept defeat. God used Churchill in a mighty way.

"I would say to the House, as I said to those who have joined this Government: "I have nothing to offer but blood, toil, tears and sweat."

We have before us an ordeal of the most grievous kind. We have before us many, many long months of struggle and of suffering.

You ask, what is our policy? I will say: It is to wage war, by sea, land, and air, with all our might and with all the strength that God can give us; to wage war against a monstrous tyranny, never surpassed in the dark, lamentable catalogue of human crime. That is our policy.

You ask, what is our aim? I answer in one word: Victory—victory at all costs, victory in spite of all terror, victory, however long and hard the road may be; for without victory, there is no survival. Let that be realized; no survival for the British Empire; no survival for all that the British Empire has stood for, no survival for the urge and impulse of the ages, that mankind will move forward towards its goal.

But I take up my task with buoyancy and hope. I feel sure that our cause will not be suffered to fail among men. At this time, I feel entitled to claim the aid of all, and I say, "Come, then, let us go forward together with our united strength."

Winston Churchill—May 10, 1940
Speech to the House of Commons

In addition to being an uncompromising, positive leader, Winston Churchill respected the Jewish people, and he loved England.

chapter 10

Safer In Blackpool

Because the city of Liverpool is a seaport, it was continually under siege. The Nazis continued to bomb as soon as darkness fell. We lived nightly with blackouts and bombings.

One evening, a portion of our home was hit by a bomb. Gratefully, our entire family was safe inside the shelter, but still it was too dangerous to stay in Liverpool. We decided to move farther north, temporarily, to Blackpool, to avoid being under constant attack.

At the Liverpool and Manchester Railway Station, we boarded the train to Blackpool, a seaside resort city located 37 kilometers (23 miles) north of Liverpool.

Since Blackpool is much smaller than Liverpool, it was not a nightly target of bombings. No military personnel were stationed there.

We rented a home and breathed a bit easier, feeling less tension without nightly attacks.

Life in Blackpool was less stressful, though war was still the reality and occasional Nazi bombings occurred. Rarely, though, were we forced to run for shelter. We slept in our beds most nights.

I immediately found employment and my family members looked after John, who was the joy of my life and the delight of their lives. Father and my siblings adored John.

Every day I hurried home from work to see John's cute face, curly brown hair and big brown eyes. His face lit up when he saw me. I immediately picked him up to tickle him and give him a hug, and he would giggle.

Previously in Liverpool, I had attended dances but did not date. One night at the ballroom I met a young Danish sailor named Frits Ove Nielsen. He spoke no English, I spoke no Danish, yet somehow we managed to communicate.

Like many sailors docking in Liverpool, Frits wanted to meet girls, so he attended dances at the Grafton Ballroom. He danced well.

Frits wanted to date me. He told a friend of mine that he loved my dark hair. Though flattered, I was at first reluctant. We knew little about each other.

In time we began dating, though Frits was unaware of my past. I did not share it with him.

In the interim, while Frits was sent out to sea, my family had moved to Blackpool. On ship he determined to learn English. The chief purser taught him enough English to correspond with me by letter.

Though I was cautious about trusting a man again, I felt somewhat at ease concerning him and mailed him a photo of me that he requested. I was rather smitten with this foreigner who seemed to adore me.

After one episode I began trusting him completely.

A friend of mine, an English sailor, met Frits at a bar while both of their ships were docked in Johannesburg, South Africa. The friend asked Frits if he was looking for a girl. Showing him my photo, Frits replied, *"I already have one."*

My friend recognized me. When the story was relayed back to me, I knew Frits was a man I could trust.

When he arrived back at port in Liverpool, Frits boarded the train north to Blackpool and we began to date again. I was still cautious of falling in love again.

Frits told me he wanted to marry me. I told him, *"There is something about me I have not told you."*

"Whatever it is does not matter. I love you," he replied.

I knew that he truly loved me. It was quite evident his feelings were genuine. I also had fallen in love with him and knew I could trust him as an honest man.

I took Frits home to meet my family. They were gracious and kind to him as he spoke broken English.

Then I told him the little boy playing was my son. He did not believe me. So I called John and said, *"Johnny, who am I?"*

John exclaimed, *"Mommy!"*

Frits looked at me incredulously, wide-eyed, and I thought, "This is more than he bargained for!"

Yet Frits promised if I married him, he would love and raise John as his own son. Anticipating a future filled with ambivalent feelings, I told him, *"If you mistreat John, it will end our relationship."*

Frits replied, *"I will love and raise John as my own son."*

Frits and I were married in Blackpool in October, 1942.

At a wedding—Sybil, Me, Frits, friend Jessie, John

Me with John, in later years

Frits was charming to everyone. Though communication in English was challenging for him, he was always a gentleman. Every family member graciously gave him time to formulate his sentences and convey his words without interrupting him. He possessed an affable nature.

My family loved Frits. He was a good husband, considerate and affectionate, and a good father to John.

Frits loved me, and I grew to love him more and more, though not without complications as in every marriage. Every time there was an issue involving John, I felt conflicted and caught in the middle between Frits and John. I knew how I wanted to raise John. Frits and John, jealous of each other, both vied for my attention.

In 1944, Frits was back at sea. Because the Nazis were engaged in war with many more countries than England, there was a reprise from their bombings on Liverpool, which was now a safer place to live.

My family left Blackpool and returned home to Liverpool. With Frits at sea, I returned to live with Madge's family on Melville Place once again, and to work at the Greek restaurant.

After several months of sailing, Frits came home on leave. I became pregnant. Our son, Peter, was born on June 9, 1946.

The war finally ended and Frits finished his sailing contract with Maersk. He returned to Liverpool to commence our future as a family.

denmark

chapter 11

Denmark—My Husband's Homeland

My husband, Frits Ove Nielsen, was born in a small, peaceful fishing village on the island of Moen in Denmark, in late 1919. Moen is close to Copenhagen and is known for its white vertical chalk cliffs.

Frits, the youngest of his family, had a twin sister, Asse, and three older brothers.

As the only girl in the family, Asse was the favored child among her siblings and parents. Asse was stronger than Frits, whom his family called "Ove" after his middle name.

As the youngest, smallest, and physically weakest family member, Frits was taunted by his brothers. This caused him to feel insecure. He consequently developed a negative attitude; a pessimistic view about life in general.

Though Frits loved his country, he longed to get away from his family. His very strict father wanted him to apprentice to be a woodcutter.

With the desire to leave family behind, 15-year old Frits visited an aunt in Copenhagen. She knew many shipping lines and sea captains. Frits asked her for assistance in getting him a job at sea. She complied.

Frits was hired as a sailor on the Maersk lines, a very large fleet with numerous merchant and naval ships. Maersk sailed all over the world and was known for their massive fleet and financial wealth. Their ships were often targeted by pirates.

Although his first voyages were difficult and Frits was seasick, he refused to go home and face his father. So he persevered. He remained a seaman until the war ended.

When I first met Frits at the Grafton Ballroom, he was on shore leave from his merchant ship that was bringing cheeses, butter, and other dairy produce, along with bacon and sausages, from Denmark to Liverpool.

As the war lingered, Frits sailed many times between Denmark and England. Once, in the midst of war, his ship left port in Liverpool for Copenhagen sailing straight north on a much longer course than usual, in an effort to avoid German battleships.

Approximately half-way of their journey, the Captain called the crew together for an announcement. He told his men that King Christian of Denmark informed his subjects that Germany was preparing to walk into Denmark and take over Copenhagen harbor.

King Christian requested all citizens with available fishing boats meet at night at a proposed secret harbor. During the night, over seven thousand Jews were transported by Danish fishing boats to Sweden, a neutral country.

My father-in-law had a couple of fishing boats. He met with other Danes that night and transported Jews to Sweden.

This was a small but important part of the World War II, and very significant to me. Indeed, the Nielsen family assisted my Jewish brethren.

I believe the Lord was in control of it all and King Christian was also a part of God's plan. God used King Christian to save thousands of Jews.

On Frits' ship, the Captain told the crew they had a decision to make; either return to Liverpool and sail under the British flag, or return to Copenhagen to be taken over by Germany. After the Captain took a vote, the vast majority wanted to return to Liverpool and sail for Britain. They sailed under the British flag until the end of World War II.

My husband survived many perilous encounters at sea, often questioning whether he would make it. Sometimes the crew changed ships mid-ocean and Frits never knew why.

Wages for seamen under the British flag were much lower than under the Danish flag. After the war ended, Denmark gave all the Danish seamen the difference in pay.

Above all, Frits was grateful to have survived the war, but it was great to receive the additional compensation from the Danish government, who took care to provide for their own citizens. This was an added bonus.

God blessed Denmark and the Danish people. I bless Denmark and the Danish people!

Just as Denmark fought to save Jews, later I would fight a spiritual battle for my Jewish brethren through my prayer ministry. In time, I learned praying for my Jewish brethren and the Nations is the Lord's purpose for my life; praying that all might accept the Messiah Jesus as Lord and Savior.

Since the war was over, I told Frits I would be happy to move to Denmark. I appreciated all they did to help my fellow Jews during the war.

However, Frits did not want to return to his homeland without employment and be at the mercy of his family for living accommodations. Jobs would be scarce, as many other returning sailors would be seeking employment.

Together we decided to make our home in Liverpool, England. We were happy with our decision.

chapter 12

Our Life In Liverpool

In Liverpool, life was returning to a new normal. Though finances were tight for everyone, England lived with an attitude of thanksgiving because the war had ended. Still, with great loss there is much depression. It took time for people to emotionally heal. Many had lost loved ones.

Frits and I faced many decisions regarding our income and living arrangements.

Because he spoke inadequate English, I realized it would be difficult for Frits to work for someone else. We needed to own a business.

The responsibility for finding a shop to open, arrange housing, etc., fell on my shoulders. Fortunately my education and determination made this feasible.

Small business loans in those days were non-existent. We had only a little working capital. I contacted a wealthy cousin for a loan but he refused.

So in 1947, along with our friends—Harry and May—we became business partners and opened a Fish and Chips Restaurant on St. James Street at Liverpool Dock Roads. Frits and I lived with our sons in an apartment above the restaurant.

This poor neighborhood on the dock road was a bad business location. Eventually we sold the shop and split the proceeds with our partners.

We needed a new opportunity. After weeks of searching we opened a new fish and chips shop. The area we selected was underdeveloped and needed capital. My sister, Sybil and her Scottish husband, Lorne Smith, became business partners with us. We named our new shop the Viking Café, after Frits' heritage.

This restaurant on Park Road was another poor location. Frits and I had a falling out with Sybil and Lorne, a disagreement about management styles and responsibilities in this failing venture. We lost the business.

Next, we opened a fish market on West Derby Road. Finally, with a great location on a busy corner, we had a successful enterprise. We bought fresh catches from fishermen and sold the fish the same day.

With revenue from this business we were able to save money. We bought a home. God blessed us with another son, Paul Henning, born August 13, 1948.

My heart's desire was the same as many women—a home, children, and a good life. We had three sons, a home and a successful business. Life was good.

chapter 13

From England To Canada

After accumulating some wealth, Frits and I decided to move our family to North America, specifically to Ontario, Canada, where Frits' brother lived with his wife and six children. This turned out to be another mistake.

We lived in a tent for several months, swatting huge mosquitoes and fighting the inclement weather of this northern latitude. I was disillusioned and miserable.

Frits' brother and family lived in the wilderness. His wife was willing to live with little or no earthly goods and raise her children in the back woods. Their home lacked modern conveniences and didn't even have screens on the windows. Amazingly, she was contented with her life.

Unlike my sister-in-law, I was not. Some women are docile and take orders well. I am not one of those women. Generally I know what I want. I grew impatient sitting by the wayside while Frits determined what he wanted to do with the rest of his life. I was unwilling to keep waiting.

After several months, I had quite enough of living in a tent with no modern amenities. When the men went to the local bar, as was their custom, the women stayed home. One day I played a different role.

Dressed in my sexiest outfit, I went to the bar. Frits was shocked when I walked in. In the presence of everyone, I told Frits I was leaving for Brooklyn, New York.

My sister, Pearl, and her husband, Bob, were willing to sponsor our family of five to come to the United States of America, and I was ready. I told Frits he could either come or stay, but I was taking our sons.

Two days later we all left Canada for Brooklyn, New York. From my perspective, it was a great decision. Frits was quietly cool.

chapter 14

Coming To America On The Fourth Of July

When we arrived in New York in 1953, it was the 4th of July. I will never forget the experience! It was destiny that we arrived on Independence Day.

All of New York was celebrating the holiday. How excited I was to be out of our tent home and in America—in New York City!

Our accommodations in Brooklyn, though far better than Canada, had drawbacks. We lived on a dirt road in a very large, one-room apartment above a clothing factory owned by my sister, Pearl and brother-in-law, Bob. The boys loved playing with their cousin David; Pearl and Bob's son.

In England, I was accustomed to paved roads. Leaving the rural area of Ontario and now living on a dirt road which was muddy when it rained, was very disappointing.

As you can imagine, five people living in one large room with no air conditioning in the middle of a hot summer was not an ideal setup. But it was a great improvement over our Canadian 'home.'

I learned the public transportation routes of New York City very quickly. Next I interviewed for, was offered, and accepted three jobs. Their locations in adjoining boroughs required me to travel for as long as two hours between shifts.

Shopping for food and schlepping it on public transportation was difficult but somehow I managed. I recall how awkward it was to carry a large brown grocery sack in each arm, while commuting on mass transit.

Fortunately, our sons adapted well to life in the United States. Frits, however, did not. He disliked the noise and fast pace of New York, though he found employment immediately. Life in the city moved rapidly. It was far busier than Liverpool.

Paul and Peter as young lads

Within a few months we were able to lease our own apartment. Eventually we purchased a small home for our family on Long Island, where our sons attended public school. It was a newly built, ranch style home in Old Bethpage.

Our lives were typical of many American households. I really enjoyed living in our new country. I enjoyed being a "typical" family.

Soon after our move to Long Island, Frits unfortunately contracted tuberculosis and was hospitalized in a sanitarium in Nassau County for almost two years.

During his hospitalization, I carried the entire physical and financial burdens for our family. It was daunting.

Eventually Frits was released from the sanitarium but he was weak and physically unable to work for several months. He rested at home for a lengthy period of time.

We had little food. When I prepared the family meal, I waited to see if there were any leftovers on the plates for me. No one noticed that I was not eating.

Through my utter exhaustion I continued to work several jobs to keep us afloat. I couldn't keep up financially so we sold the home and took a loss on the sale. We paid back the mortgage loan and rented an apartment close to my sister Sybil, and brother-in-law Lorne, in Long Beach.

Peter was in high school and Paul was in middle school. John graduated from high school and enrolled in Hofstra University on Long Island.

chapter 19

Problems In Our Marriage

Progressively we struggled in our marriage.

Frits attended a cosmetology/barber school and became a hairdresser. He partnered in a salon with a gay stylist. Frits was drinking a lot of alcohol and partying with his business partner and other gay men. He was staying out long hours.

John was dating gay men, though I didn't know it at the time. Frits knew but didn't tell me.

One of my jobs was working at a kosher delicatessen. The Jewish owner sympathized with me and my plight. Our emotions took over and we had an affair.

All the employees of the deli knew about the affair, including the owner's wife, who also worked at the establishment. She didn't mention my relationship with her husband but when she looked at me, her expression said everything.

I had fallen in love with this man. My heart believed he loved me and would divorce his spouse to marry me.

It would never happen.

My boss had no intention of anything more than an affair. He said that he would buy me an apartment and take care of me.

I was *not* looking to be a mistress. What a painful lesson! How disillusioned I was.

My husband learned of the intricate affair. Frits pleaded with me to end it. Fortunately, I was sensible enough to resign the job at the deli and entirely leave this relationship.

Quite obviously this was a major marital crisis. After the affair ended, Frits and I finally began to communicate, coming to an understanding about our marriage.

Frits told me how much he hated living the fast pace of New York. We decided to leave Long Island, get a fresh start on our marriage, and move to a new city in a new state. I was also tired of dealing with multiple jobs in the congestion of New York City.

California was especially appealing because I dreamed of the rich life which made that state famous. Frits was lured west by the promise of warmer weather and open spaces.

By the time we planned the transcontinental move, Peter was away at college in Boston. Because he is an incredibly talented artist, he had been awarded an art scholarship to Emerson College in Massachusetts.

Though he moved on campus immediately following his high school graduation, Peter did not stay at Emerson. He had not developed the discipline and study habits to succeed in college.

Peter opted to return home and move with our family out West. Later he attended junior college in California with much better success than at Emerson.

Paul was a junior in high school when we decided to move. He was extremely unhappy to be leaving his classmates and friends in Long Island.

John was already out in the world on his own and living a successful lifestyle. He opted to stay in New York. He had moved to Manhattan after college and worked in retail clothing at Brooks Brothers.

Tall and trim with dark wavy hair, John looked like a model. He was handsome, suave, and debonair. The management at Brooks Brothers said he was like a walking advertisement for their clothes.

chapter 16

California Living

Frits and I, along with Peter and Paul, settled in Santa Monica, California and lived in a three bedroom apartment above a shop named the Chinese General Store. Frits and I managed the shop for the owner, who was a delightful lady. We loved the job and it provided us with a good income.

As a couple, Frits and I had experienced many challenges together. There had been good times, but our marriage also had many trials and disappointments. I wanted to divorce. Frits did not.

As with many couples who must make that decision for themselves and their families, we decided our sons gave us reason to stay together. We both loved them with all our hearts and this was the right decision for us.

Frits and I loved our location, so we bought a home in Santa Monica. We opened a franchise restaurant named British Fish and Chips. Eventually we sold this and opened another restaurant named the 'Viking Café,' after Frits' heritage.

How ironic that later I would live in Scandinavian Minnesota and become a Vikings football fan!

Throughout my life I have never driven a car and never had a license to drive, but in sprawling California, we needed a car. We bought a Volkswagen which Frits drove. He loved it.

This was the first time Frits enjoyed living in America. He seemed to be genuinely happy. Paul and Peter also got their drivers licenses so they could chauffeur me to work.

Peter's first job in Santa Monica was working at a picture frame factory. Later he was hired by Douglas Aircraft, which became McDonald Douglas.

After a traffic accident in a California canyon, Peter was given a citation. The other driver took us to court and the citation stayed on Peter's record. This prevented him from being drafted into the U.S. Army when America was fighting combat in the Vietnam War.

Peter married a Jewish girl named Sue. They moved to Spain and were together for 18 years before their marriage ended.

Paul finished the last two years of high school and then enrolled in UCLA. While in college, he received a military draft notification from the U.S. Army.

Along with many UCLA students during this era, Paul was a conscientious objector. He decided to leave America and return to England, his birthplace. He had dual citizenship.

In London, Paul met his future wife, Carol, a devastated young widow whose husband had died on a battlefield in Vietnam.

John left his position at Brooks Brothers in Manhattan and moved to the Bahamas, a British colony. For several years he lived there, basking in the relaxing island lifestyle. Eventually he moved to California and married a woman named Pam. They had one son. Later they divorced and John returned to the gay lifestyle.

These years in California were good for Frits and me and our marriage.

Frits and Me in California

A Visiting English Tour Bus
In front of "British Fish & Chips"

Isle of Wight

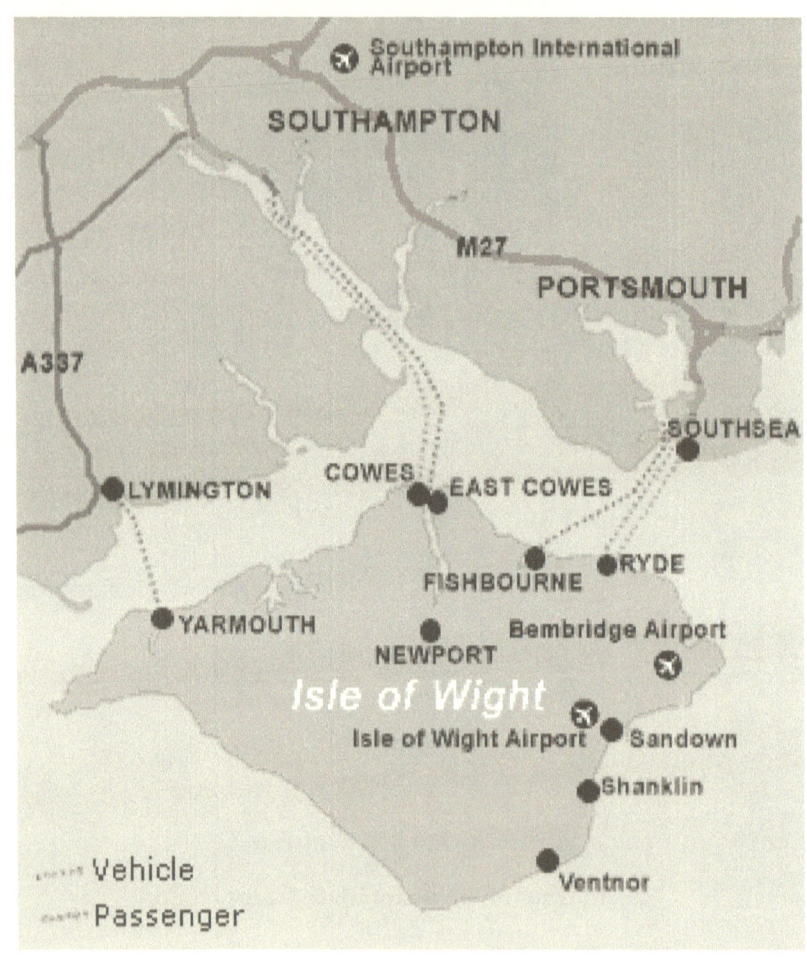

chapter 17

Back To England

Even though the pace of California was slower than New York, Frits still longed to return to England. Our sons were grown, so we sold our possessions and moved to the Isle of Wight at the southernmost tip of Great Britain. It is detached from the mainland.

We longed for countryside serenity and avoided Liverpool, which had become very congested and industrialized.

The beautiful Isle of Wight had been home to poet Alfred Lord Tennyson, and summer home to Queen Victoria. Many sailing regattas occur there each summer.

My sister, Sybil, was living in Florida and had been recently widowed. Mourning her husband and feeling quite melancholy, she also longed to return home to Britain.

In partnership with Sybil, Frits and I bought a home and settled in for a slower paced lifestyle. We bought another Volkswagen and spent the first winter there.

Indeed, the Isle of Wight is very lovely and serene with a much slower pace. This was the dead of winter, however, and there was no available work.

After staying for two years, we sold our home. Sybil decided to return to Florida. She had two children living in the United States.

Frits and I were unsure of our future. Where should we go? Friends in Florida called and told us to come back to America. Since two of my sisters, Sybil and Pearl, lived in Florida, we decided relocating back to America would be a logical choice.

Our home on the Isle of Wight

chapter 18

Life In The Sunshine State

After returning to the U.S., Frits and I first moved to the east coast of Florida and then to the west coast of Florida and were eventually all over the map in that state. We just couldn't seem to settle in and find our niche.

Yet in whatever city we landed in that state, both Frits and I always found employment; he as a cook and I as a waitress.

In multiple cities throughout Florida, Frits and I lived in apartments, worked various jobs, and saved our money. We decided to build a new ranch home on the west coast of Florida, on the gulf side.

Back in England, Paul and Carol had fallen in love, married, and had two children. With 2-year old Elise and 6-month old Paul, Jr., they used the widow's pension Carol had received from the death of her first husband to move to Spain, where Carol's sister lived.

In Spain, Paul was unable to find work, so we sent money to him regularly. We advised him to leave Spain and return to the U.S., where he could support his family.

Paul and Carol accepted our advice, so we financed the trip for their family of four to fly to Florida. They arrived in the United States as hippies, owning nothing but the clothing on their backs.

At this point in time, the construction of our pristine home was near completion. Yet we would not be first to occupy this lovely home. We allowed Paul and Carol and their children to move in while Frits and I stayed in our rented apartment. It seemed logical since they were a family of four and we were a family of two.

Soon the new home was beginning to show wear, being occupied by a young family with small children.

To complicate the situation, Carol and I did not agree on methods of housekeeping and raising children. Paul was in the habit of receiving our financial support.

Frits and I began to resent our sacrifice. We had strong disagreements with Paul and Carol at this time.

Paul and Carol possessed relaxed, easy-going personalities. They were hippies. Frits also possessed a mellow personality. I, however, have always been more structured and intense, always setting goals and making commitments. All of us developed a strained relationship with one another.

In Florida, Paul eventually found work in a boat yard. Since he didn't own a car, we helped the couple find an apartment close enough to Paul's employment for him to walk to work, so their family could move out of the ranch home.

Frits and I then moved into our new home, but it never really felt like our home and it was difficult to settle in. Eventually we decided to sell it and relocate back to California, and gain a fresh new start.

chapter 19

Back To California

Of all the places Frits and I lived in America, California was our favorite. We felt drawn back to the wide open spaces and sunny days. The atmosphere in California was more relaxed than anywhere we had lived, and the humidity level was lower, making it easier for Frits to breathe.

Paul and Carol did not want to stay in Florida without us. So both couples sold most of our possessions and loaded a rented trailer with our remaining belongings. Along with the children, Elise and Paul, Jr., all six of us drove by car to Lake Tahoe, California.

Three months after living in Lake Tahoe, we returned to Santa Monica and bought a home just four blocks from the Pacific Ocean. Though Lake Tahoe is lovely, our favorite city, Santa Monica, beckoned us to return.

In a nearby hippie neighborhood, Paul and Carol rented an apartment. Paul immediately found employment and Carol gave birth to their third child, a daughter they named Christine.

Frits and I stayed in Santa Monica for a couple of years. But since I have a bit of wanderlust in my soul, the two of us were ready to move back to Florida.

chapter 20

To Florida, And My Husband's Death

In 1983, we moved to the West Coast of Florida and bought a condo in Tarpon Springs. I found work at a delicatessen.

The tuberculosis my husband suffered earlier in our marriage had weakened Frits and left him in poor health, vulnerable to chronic illnesses. After two years of living in Florida, he passed away.

I was quite distressed. Our marriage had grown stronger and I hadn't contemplated being widowed. Yet I was also relieved not to nurse Frits and his sicknesses.

Soon after my husband's death, I found a position near Clearwater as a food service supervisor at an upscale retirement community named Mease Manor. The pay was good and allowed me to live a carefree lifestyle.

After years of taking care of my family, I began to enjoy my independence and only having responsibility to take care of myself.

Living as a single, widowed woman for several years, I embraced the opportunity to enjoy life. Cruise vacations were my luxury of choice. I sailed 22 times and had frequent customer cards from all the major cruise lines.

My oldest son, John, was now single and living in Florida. He was gay and had a partner.

John and his partner decided, and I agreed, to pool our money together to build a lovely home with a mother-in-law's wing. I put my entire savings into the new home, everything I had.

Near the end process of this construction venture, all three of us embarked on a cruise to celebrate the "almost completed" construction of our new home.

One evening on the cruise ship, John did not come to dinner. His partner came to the table and told me that he and John decided together it was not going to work for me to live with them.

I was devastated.

There I was, in the middle of the ocean, with a broken heart and am empty savings account. All of the years of my diligent saving were lost.

Immediately I told the ship's Captain I needed to disembark at the next port of call. Though this is a nearly impossible task, the Captain radioed ahead and allowed me to disembark on the island of Martinique. From there I flew back to Florida on my own.

Leaving a ship in the midst of a cruise requires much paperwork and final approval from the U.S. government.

Feeling rejected by my own son and penniless, the words of John's partner played in my mind. I was hurt even more because John didn't have the courage to tell me of their change of plans, but rather had his partner convey their decision to me.

On the mainland, I told my sisters what had transpired on the cruise. Pearl invited me to move in with her and her husband until I could get back on my feet.

Once more, living with family was difficult. I felt more like Pearl's child than her sister. Both Pearl and Bob were so kind to me, but she was accustomed to plating and serving Bob his meals and so she plated and served my meals, also.

What a dilemma I was in at this latter stage of my life.

I spoke on the phone with my son, Paul, who had relocated to Minnesota. He suggested I come up north to live close to him and Carol and their children and grandchildren.

I prayed, *"Dear God, Minnesota! Where is that on the map? It might as well be Siberia!"*

Finally in desperation, I agreed to move north to Minnesota, the 'land of 10,000 lakes.'

chapter 21

A New Chapter Of Life With My Family

My relocation to the state of Minnesota is probably my final and most important move, designed by God from the beginning of creation, for no decision in my life could compare to the one I made while living here.

In Minnesota, at 83 years of age, I finally recognized my Messiah! God led me *"beside the still waters,"* as stated in the 23rd Psalm. My life changed forever.

Though Minnesota winters can be lengthy and harsh, replete with bitter cold and snow, summer weather is all the more precious, lending itself to opportunities of fellowship with family and friends. The hearts of Minnesotans are warm and welcoming all year round, and the love of God is prevalent in their inviting ways.

After I ceased my inner rebellion toward God for having me relocate to the frozen tundra, I recognized the quality of life here is priceless. Did you know that Minnesota was the first state to ban smoking at our international airport and in public places? It is a healthy state that encourages healthy lifestyles. People love God and country. They cherish the U.S. Constitution and the Bill of Rights.

So in Minnesota, Paul secured a lovely one-bedroom apartment for me in a Jewish high rise named Menorah West, at the Ackerberg Community Complex on Philips Parkway, located in the Minneapolis suburb of St. Louis Park.

Paul is a wonderful son. He chauffeurs me wherever I need to go and conscientiously sees that all of my needs are met.

Paul and Carol had become believers in Yeshua ha Mashiach—Jesus the Messiah, in the early 1990s. They attended a church in Mound, the suburb where they lived, and often invited me to attend Sunday services with them. Since I longed to be with family, I tagged along.

One Sunday morning at the church in Mound, I listened to the message. The pastor quoted Micah 5:2, and spoke of how the Messiah is prevalent throughout Scripture, if you only look for Him.

With a humble heart, I asked God for His forgiveness, and invited Jesus into my heart.

Wow! It was amazing! The Ruach ha Kodesh—the Holy Spirit—came into my heart and changed me from within. This is the most profound, life-changing experience I have known! I now belong to the Son of God!

Worship at the Mound church was enriching and edifying, yet because of my heritage, I longed to worship at a Jewish synagogue where people know Jesus as their Messiah.

Paul and Carol took me to the Seed of Abraham, a Messianic synagogue located in St. Louis Park, the suburb where I now live.

Rabbi Ed Rothman was so kind to me and was amazed that God called me to be born again at age 83! He and Paul became good friends and for a period of time, Paul even served as an elder at this congregation.

Because of my request to Rabbi Ed Rothman and the pastor from Mound, one Sunday afternoon they immersed (baptized) me in Lake Minnetonka, a large Minnesota lake in the Twin Cities metropolitan area.

Since that time 13 years ago, I have been a member of Seed of Abraham and worship at their services. I serve my Master by leading the prayer ministry and assigning weekly Torah readers. With great joy, I am an intercessor in prayer to my Savior and Lord, Jesus—the Messiah.

The blessings of my life are abundant. My spiritual needs are met and my physical needs are met.

My apartment is lovely and my furnishings are contemporary, very 21st Century.

From a menu where I select my personal choices, kosher lunch and dinner meals are delivered to me daily by the Roitenberg Kitchens. I prepare my own breakfast.

Being British by birth, I do enjoy my tea, which I always drink with milk. That keeps my bones strong. I also have a penchant for dark chocolate. It has anti-oxidants, you know.

A shopper comes to my home weekly and uses a list I provide to purchase goods for my use.

Cheryl, my dear hairdresser friend, comes right to my home to shampoo and style my hair. We share a deep love of our Messiah.

My weekly laundry is completed and my apartment is cleaned by a lady who visits me from Jewish Family Services.

You see, God provides for all my needs.

Plus, it is such a joy to live close to family. Paul and Carol and their children and families treat me so well, inviting me to every holiday and family event. We even take annual vacations along the North Shore by Lake Superior.

A beautiful point on Lake Superior

chapter 22

My Beloved Family

My older son, Peter, has lived in Spain for 40 years. Following the end of his first marriage, he met a lovely British lady named Gillian. They were both guests at a dinner party at the home of a friend. Gillian's marriage had also ended and she and Peter had many mutual friends.

At the time they met, Peter was teaching Gill's children in the Spanish village of Mijas on the Mediterranean Sea. He taught science, math, physical education and drama.

Eventually, Peter and Gillian married. They have been together 20 years.

In a small village not far from the university city of Coimbra, Portugal, Peter and Gillian are building a new home. The city is located in a beautiful location of valued history.

Using the original 350 year old walls for the exterior of the compound, they are building the entire interior from the ground up. Peter is doing the work himself and hopes to finish within five years.

Peter and Gillian have a great marriage, one where they have both been able to grow in understanding and happiness. Praise the Lord for the gift of love!

Peter is a good supporter of Gillian's endeavors as an antiques dealer and writer. Gillian's support has enabled Peter to approach artwork full-time in painting, sculpting, and other fine art disciplines.

Throughout his lifetime, Peter has earned a living as a teacher, plumber, electrician, carpenter, builder, etc. He has always been able to exhibit his art but previously worked at it part-time.

I am so blessed because each summer, Peter visits me in Minnesota. Last year, Gillian also traveled here to Minnesota, for the first time. Since I know she doesn't care for flying, I am thrilled she made an exception so we could meet in person. Gillian promises to return to Minnesota for my 100th birthday.

Gillian and Peter and I keep in touch with regular email and occasional phone conversations.

Peter is a good son.

Peter visiting me from Spain

My younger son, Paul, is an excellent businessman in Minneapolis, the Vice President of a large millwork company. His wife, Carol, is retired.

Paul and Carol now worship as members of the Basilica of St. Mary, a large Roman Catholic Church in Minneapolis. The joy of knowing our Messiah is realizing that denominations are immaterial. What matters is that Jesus lives in our hearts.

We are blessed that Paul and Carol have three beautiful children with lovely families who all live in the Minneapolis suburban area. I am thrilled to enjoy seven wonderful great-grandchildren.

All of Paul's family are so good to me, inviting me to every family event but gracious enough to allow me to choose according to my interests and energy levels.

Life for me is filled with faith, family, and friends. How great to enjoy wonderful sons and daughters-in-law, and beautiful grandchildren and great-grandchildren. My cup is full. I am so grateful to God!

My one regret is that I never spoke to my oldest son, John, after the Caribbean cruise. I sent many letters to him in Florida but they were returned to me, unopened.

My youngest sister, Pearl, aged 91, is living in Florida. We stay in touch. She is my only living sibling. Her son, my nephew David, also stays in touch with me. He and his wife live in New York where he works in the financial industry. They recently hosted Peter and Paul, who were visiting New York while on a nostalgia tour to reminisce growing up on Long Island during their school age years.

God even brought my extended family back into my life. Sybil's daughter, niece Janice Grant, emails me regularly and delighted me with a surprise visit to Minnesota last summer with her husband, Lawrence.

I have also connected with some of Frits' relatives in Denmark.

My life is richly blessed with good health, great family, dear friends, and my everlasting faith in God.

My dear friend, Jackie Garamella, has been wonderful through the years. She drives me to synagogue and medical appointments.

Through His incredible love, Jesus, my Messiah, drew me to Himself. He didn't force me to love Him but gently called my name. Though late in life, I eventually surrendered my pride and stubbornness and received His forgiveness and salvation. Now I am free! Halleluiah!

Whenever I even hear the name of Jesus, every cell in my body rejoices. He is the lover of my soul.

Whether you say Jesus or in Hebrew, Yeshua (meaning Messiah or Savior), I love to hear His name.

chapter 23

A Special Guest Speaker

Frequently, Seed of Abraham invites guest speakers. In the cold Minnesota winter of 2004, Dr. Howard Morgan, from Duluth, Georgia, spoke at Shabbat. He was dynamic. On this frigid January day, to the amusement of the congregation, Dr. Morgan joked,

"I say, 'Thank You, Thank You, Thank You, God, that I am living in Duluth, Georgia and not Duluth, Minnesota.'"

Our congregation laughed heartily.

Dr. Morgan has a global ministry with offices in the U.S. and England. He mixes humor with profound messages and is an incredibly effective speaker.

After the service, I told Dr, Morgan how much I enjoyed his message. He thanked me and replied, *"You have an interesting accent. Are you English?"*

I said, *"Yes, I was born in Liverpool."*

Dr. Morgan said, *"I was born in Liverpool!"*

I told him, *"I lived on Bamber Street."*

Dr. Morgan said, *"I lived on Bamber Street!!!"*

We were both quite amazed. When Dr. Morgan told me his mother's name, I was really excited. His mother lived across the street from me and we had been playmates as children.

Now Dr. Morgan describes our encounter to others saying, *"I was blown away!"*

Isn't it phenomenal the way God weaves an intricate tapestry, intertwining us with others we meet along our life's path? The connections are amazing!

Dr. Morgan and his lovely wife, Janet, have a special place in my heart.

Rabbi Edwin Rothman, Senior Rabbi of Seed of Abraham Messianic Congregation

Dr. Howard Morgan of Howard Morgan Ministries, Atlanta, Georgia, U.S.A. and Birkenhead, Wirral, England

Rabbi Bruce Niger, Associate Rabbi of Seed of Abraham Messianic Congregation

(Rabbi Bruce is a former OB/GYN physician)

chapter 24

My Ministry In His Earthly Kingdom

God gave me a wonderful ministry, and I am privileged to serve Him. It is an honor for me to pray and intercede for His people.

As leader of the prayer chain at the Seed of Abraham Messianic Congregation, many people are amazed that at 96 years young, I use a computer and send out email prayer requests.

Computers are a technological wonder. They are a great tool to magnify His holy name throughout the earth. I marvel at God and all He allowed mankind to design and build.

I encourage others to always, always be positive, and *"Never stop learning."*

God blessed me so much throughout my life, and the past 13 years have been amazing.

- I enjoyed a trip to my beloved Israel through the gracious generosity of many wonderful people
- I was maid of honor at the wedding of dear friends, Marilyn and Patrick Freeman *(imagine that, a bridesmaid at age 86!)*
- I have lit candles and prayed Hebrew blessings for many organizations, congregations, and in my own home and the home of many friends
- I have spoken before many congregations and organizations to honor my Lord and Messiah, Yeshua

- I have entertained wonderful believers in my home throughout the years in Minnesota, and been a guest of in the homes of many fellow believers
- I have prayed intercessory prayers for many people and causes

I am most amazed our awesome Abba Father would love us so much, that He would allow His only Son to take our sins and save us for all eternity. As the mother of three sons, I can scarcely imagine this incredible unselfish Love. It is all powerful . . . a selfless sacrifice.

Jesus is Lord! Jesus is *my* Lord! I love Him, the lover of my soul. Halleluiah!

So this day, I invite you, my friend, to invite Jesus into your heart.

I encourage you to ask Him to redeem your sins. Whether Jew or Gentile, He invites all to receive His love and forgiveness.

Since death is imminent for all mankind, at the risk of being homiletic, may I suggest you read some powerful Scripture to enlighten your soul and enrich your mind?

Read the 9th chapter of the book of Daniel. Imagine yourself standing before the "Ancient of Days."

Read Isaiah 59, and consider God's gift of His Son. Read Isaiah 53, and consider His suffering.

Then read the words of John 17, the actual "Lord's prayer," where Jesus prayed for His disciples and for future posterity. Jesus actually prayed for you, dear friend!

Please consider making Yeshua your Lord and Savior, so that if I don't meet you here on earth, I will meet you in the heavenly Kingdom. The choice is all yours.

Let's enjoy an incredible eternity together, worshiping the Creator of the Universe!

Shalom, dear friend! Shalom!

Celebrating Sukkot with dear friend and Seed of Abraham *elder emeritus*, Helen Anderberg

"I am carrying the lulav and etrog"

Dancing under the chuppah with special friends, Karen Guimont and Jan Taylor

Lighting a Hanukkiah

Best friends, Marlene Moore and Jackie Garamella

Wedding bliss with bride friend, Marilyn Freeman

Hanukkah laughter with writer friend, CoCo Banken

Joyful summer times with editor friend, Ann Anderson

references

1. All Biblical references are from ***The Holy Scriptures,*** *and* ***The New Testament,*** publications from <u>The Society for Distributing Hebrew Scriptures, Joseph House, 1 Bury Mead Road, Hitchin, Herts. SG5 1RT ENGLAND</u> (Registered Charity No. 232692)

2. Judiac practices and procedures compiled from various internet websites or printed sources including ***The Everything Judaism Book***, by Richard Bank, Adams Media Corporation, Avon, Massachusetts, ISBN:1-58062-728-5, COPYRIGHT ©2002, <u>www.adamsmedia.com</u>

3. *<u>Fiddler on the Roof</u>* references are from the documentary, ***<u>Sholom Aleichem: Laughing in the Darkness</u>***, <u>www. MyJewishLearning.com</u>

4. Winston Churchill quote from, ***The Wit & Wisdom of Winston Churchill***, by James C. Humes, Harper Perennial, A Division of Harper Collins Publishers, 10 East 53rd Street, New York, NY 10022, ISBN:0-06-092577-9, COPYRIGHT ©1995

5. United Kingdom and Denmark maps from the United States Central Intelligence Agency website, <u>www.cia.gov</u>

6. Photographs from the personal collections of Mildred Nielsen, St. Louis Park, Minnesota, U.S.A. and CoCoCommunications, Minnetonka, Minnesota, U.S.A. or uncopyrighted internet sources.

recommended websites

- www.Aish.com
- www.Jewfaq.org
- www.AskMoses.com
- www.MyJewishLearning.com
- www.FridayLight.org
- www.chabad.org
- www.bnaibrith.org
- www.howardmorganministries.org
- www.seedofabraham.org
- www.gnfi.org
- www.mjaa.org
- www.mjcc.org